What I Saw of Shiloh

*The Memories and Experiences of
Ambrose Bierce During the
American Civil War*

D1599935

British Library Cataloguing-in-Publication Data
A catalogue record for this book is available from the
British Library

Contents

Ambrose Bierce

Ambrose Gwinnett Bierce was born in Meigs County, Ohio, United States in 1842. He was the tenth of thirteen children, and left home aged fifteen to become a 'printer's devil' (a printing apprentice) at a small Ohio newspaper. Bierce fought in the American Civil War, working as a topographical engineer and even reaching the rank of brevet major before resigning from the Army to settle in San Francisco. During the 1870s and 1880s, he worked on a variety of newspapers, even spending three years in England, and famously helped quash a bill which would have put the cost of the First Transcontinental Railroad on the American people instead of the railroad companies.

Through his newspaper output – including one of the first regular columns in William Randolph Hearst's newspaper, the San Francisco Examiner – Bierce developed a famous reputation for searing criticism and acerbic wit, even earning the nickname 'Bitter Bierce'. His satirical reference book, The Devil's Dictionary, which lampooned cant and political doublespeak – "Corporation (n.) An ingenious device for obtaining profit without individual responsibility" – remains widely read today. However, Bierce is critically best remembered for his fiction. Indeed, many of his short stories – such as 'An Occurrence at Owl Creek Bridge', 'The Boarded Window', 'Killed at Resaca' and 'Chickamauga', all of which are penned in 'Pure English' – are held among the best of the 19th century. Bierce's writings are also generally regarded as some of the best war writings of all time.

Bierce's death was a mysterious one, which continues to intrigue people to this day: In October 1913, aged 71, Bierce left Washington, D.C., for a tour of his old Civil

War battlefields. He got as far as the Mexican city of Chihuahua, where he wrote a letter to a close friend, dated 26th December, 1913, in which he said "I leave here tomorrow for an unknown destination." After this he vanished, becoming one of the most famous disappearances in American literary history.

What I Saw of Shiloh

First published in 1881.

I

This is a simple story of a battle; such a tale as may be told by a soldier who is no writer to a reader who is no soldier.

The morning of Sunday, the sixth day of April, 1862, was bright and warm. Reveille had been sounded rather late, for the troops, wearied with long marching, were to have a day of rest. The men were idling about the embers of their bivouac fires; some preparing breakfast, others looking carelessly to the condition of their arms and accoutrements, against the inevitable inspection; still others were chatting with indolent dogmatism on that never-failing theme, the end and object of the campaign. Sentinels paced up and down the confused front with a lounging freedom of mien and stride that would not have been tolerated at another time. A few of them limped unsoldierly in deference to blistered feet. At a little distance in rear of the stacked arms were a few tents out of which frowsy-headed officers occasionally peered, languidly calling to their servants to fetch a basin of water, dust a coat or polish a scabbard. Trim young mounted orderlies, bearing dispatches obviously unimportant, urged their lazy nags by devious ways amongst the men, enduring with unconcern their good-humored raillery, the penalty of superior station. Little negroes of not very clearly defined status and function lolled on their stomachs, kicking their long, bare heels in the sunshine, or slumbered peacefully, unaware of the practical waggery prepared by white hands for their undoing.

Presently the flag hanging limp and lifeless at headquarters was seen to lift itself spiritedly from the staff. At the same instant was heard a dull, distant sound like the heavy breathing of some great animal below the horizon. The flag had lifted its head to listen. There was a momentary lull in the hum of the human swarm; then, as the flag drooped the hush passed away. But there were some hundreds more men on their feet than before; some thousands of hearts beating with a quicker pulse.

Again the flag made a warning sign, and again the breeze bore to our ears the long, deep sighing of iron lungs. The division, as if it had received the sharp word of command, sprang to its feet, and stood in groups at "attention." Even the little blacks got up. I have since seen similar effects produced by earthquakes; I am not sure but the ground was trembling then. The mess-cooks, wise in their generation, lifted the steaming camp-kettles off the fire and stood by to cast out. The mounted orderlies had somehow disappeared. Officers came ducking from beneath their tents and gathered in groups. Headquarters had become a swarming hive.

The sound of the great guns now came in regular throbbings—the strong, full pulse of the fever of battle. The flag flapped excitedly, shaking out its blazonry of stars and stripes with a sort of fierce delight. Toward the knot of officers in its shadow dashed from somewhere—he seemed to have burst out of the ground in a cloud of dust—a mounted aide-de-camp, and on the instant rose the sharp, clear notes of a bugle, caught up and repeated, and passed on by other bugles, until the level reaches of brown fields, the line of woods trending away to far hills, and the unseen valleys beyond were "telling of the sound," the farther, fainter strains half drowned in ringing cheers as the men ran to range themselves behind the stacks of arms. For this call was not the wearisome "general" before which the tents go down; it was the exhilarating "assembly," which goes to the heart as wine and stirs the blood like the kisses of a beautiful woman. Who that has heard it calling to him above the grumble of great guns can forget the wild intoxication of its music?

II

The Confederate forces in Kentucky and Tennessee had suffered a series of reverses, culminating in the loss of Nashville. The blow was severe: immense quantities of war material had fallen to the victor, together with all the important strategic points. General Johnston withdrew Beauregard's army to Corinth, in northern Mississippi, where he hoped so to recruit and equip it as to enable it to assume the offensive and retake the lost territory.

The town of Corinth was a wretched place—the capital of a swamp. It is a two days' march west of the Tennessee River, which here and for a hundred and fifty miles farther, to where it falls into the Ohio at Paducah, runs nearly north. It is navigable to this point—that is to say, to Pittsburg Landing, where Corinth got to it by a road worn through a thickly wooded country seamed with ravines and bayous, rising nobody knows where and running into the river under sylvan arches heavily draped with Spanish moss. In some places they were obstructed by fallen trees. The Corinth road was at certain seasons a branch of the Tennessee River. Its mouth was Pittsburg Landing. Here in 1862 were some fields and a house or two; now there are a national cemetery and other improvements.

It was at Pittsburg Landing that Grant established his army, with a river in his rear and two toy steamboats as a means of communication with the east side, whither General Buell with thirty thousand men was moving from Nashville to join him. The question has been asked, Why did General Grant occupy the enemy's side of the river in the face of a superior force before the arrival of Buell? Buell had a long way to come; perhaps Grant was weary of waiting. Certainly Johnston was, for in the gray of the morning of April 6th, when Buell's leading division was en bivouac near the little town of Savannah, eight or ten miles below, the Confederate forces, having moved out of Corinth two days before, fell upon Grant's advance brigades and destroyed them. Grant was at Savannah, but hastened to the Landing in time to find his camps in the hands of the enemy and the remnants of his beaten army cooped up with an impassable river at their backs for moral support. I have related how the news of this affair came to us at Savannah. It came on the wind—a messenger that does not bear copious details.

III

On the side of the Tennessee River, over against Pittsburg Landing, are some low bare hills, partly inclosed by a forest. In the dusk of the evening of April 6 this open space, as seen from the other side of the stream—whence, indeed, it was anxiously watched by thousands of eyes, to many of which it grew dark long before the sun went down—would have appeared to have been ruled in long, dark lines, with new lines being constantly drawn across. These lines were the regiments of Buell's leading division, which having moved up from Savannah through a country presenting nothing but interminable swamps and pathless "bottom lands," with rank overgrowths of jungle, was arriving at the scene of action breathless, footsore and faint with hunger. It had been a terrible race; some regiments had lost a third of their number from fatigue, the men dropping from the ranks as if shot, and left to recover or die at their leisure. Nor was the scene to which they had been invited likely to inspire the moral confidence that medicines physical fatigue. True, the air was full of thunder and the earth was trembling beneath their feet; and if there is truth in the theory of the conversion of force, these men were storing up energy from every shock that burst its waves upon their bodies. Perhaps this theory may better than another explain the tremendous endurance of men in battle. But the eyes reported only matter for despair.

Before us ran the turbulent river, vexed with plunging shells and obscured in spots by blue sheets of low-lying smoke. The two little steamers were doing their duty well. They came over to us empty and went back crowded, sitting very low in the water, apparently on the point of capsizing. The farther edge of the water could not be seen; the boats came out of the obscurity, took on their passengers and vanished in the darkness. But on the heights above, the battle was burning brightly enough; a thousand lights kindled and expired in every second of time. There were broad flushings in the sky, against which the branches of the trees showed black. Sudden flames burst out here and there, singly and in dozens. Fleeting streaks of fire crossed over to us by way of welcome. These expired in blinding flashes and fierce little rolls of smoke, attended with the peculiar metallic ring of bursting shells, and followed by the musical humming of the fragments as they struck into the ground on every side, making us wince, but doing little harm. The air was full of noises. To the right and the left the musketry rattled smartly and petulantly; directly in front it sighed and growled. To the experienced ear this meant that the death-line was an arc of which the river was the chord. There were deep, shaking explosions and smart shocks; the whisper of stray bullets and the hurtle of conical shells; the rush of round shot. There were faint, desultory cheers, such as announce a momentary or partial triumph. Occasionally, against the glare behind the trees, could be seen moving black figures, singularly distinct but apparently no longer than a thumb. They seemed to me ludicrously like the figures of demons in old allegorical prints of hell. To destroy these and all their belongings the enemy needed but another hour of daylight; the steamers in that case would have been doing him fine service by bringing more fish to his net. Those of us who had the good fortune to arrive late could then have eaten our teeth in impotent rage. Nay, to make his victory sure it did not need that the sun should pause in the heavens; one of the many random shots falling into the river would have done the business had chance directed it into the engine-room of a steamer. You can perhaps fancy the anxiety with which we watched them leaping down.

But we had two other allies besides the night. Just where the enemy had pushed his right flank to the river was the mouth of a wide bayou, and here two gunboats had taken station. They too were of the toy sort, plated perhaps with railway metals, perhaps with boiler-iron. They staggered under a heavy gun or two each. The bayou made an opening in the high bank of the river. The bank was a parapet, behind which the gunboats crouched, firing up the bayou as through an embrasure. The enemy was at this disadvantage: he could not get at the gunboats, and he could advance only by exposing his flank to their ponderous missiles, one of which would have broken a half-mile of his bones and made nothing of it. Very annoying this must have been—these twenty gunners beating back an army because a sluggish creek had been pleased to fall into a river at one point rather than another. Such is the part that accident may play in the game of war.

As a spectacle this was rather fine. We could just discern the black bodies of these boats, looking very much like turtles. But when they let off their big guns there was a conflagration. The river shuddered in its banks, and hurried on, bloody, wounded, terrified! Objects a mile away sprang toward our eyes as a snake strikes at the face of its victim. The report stung us to the brain, but we blessed it audibly. Then we could hear the great shell tearing away through the air until the sound died out in the distance; then, a surprisingly long time afterward, a dull, distant explosion and a sudden silence of small-arms told their own tale.

IV

There was, I remember, no elephant on the boat that passed us across that evening, nor, I think, any hippopotamus. These would have been out of place. We had, however, a woman. Whether the baby was somewhere on board I did not learn. She was a fine creature, this woman; somebody's wife. Her mission, as she understood it, was to inspire the failing heart with courage; and when she selected mine I felt less flattered by her preference than astonished by her penetration. How did she learn? She stood on the upper deck with the red blaze of battle bathing her beautiful face, the twinkle of a thousand rifles mirrored in her eyes; and displaying a small ivory-handled pistol, she told me in a sentence punctuated by the thunder of great guns that if it came to the worst she would do her duty like a man! I am proud to remember that I took off my hat to this little fool.

V

Along the sheltered strip of beach between the river bank and the water was a confused mass of humanity—several thousands of men. They were mostly unarmed; many were wounded; some dead. All the camp-following tribes were there; all the cowards; a few officers. Not one of them knew where his regiment was, nor if he had a regiment. Many had not. These men were defeated, beaten, cowed. They were deaf to duty and dead to shame. A more demented crew never drifted to the rear of broken battalions. They would have stood in their tracks and been shot down to a man by a provost-marshal's guard, but they could not have been urged up that bank. An army's bravest men are its cowards. The death which they would not meet at the hands of the enemy they will meet at the hands of their officers, with never a flinching.

Whenever a steamboat would land, this abominable mob had to be kept off her with bayonets; when she pulled away, they sprang on her and were pushed by scores into the water, where they were suffered to drown one another in their own way. The men disembarking insulted them, shoved them, struck them. In return they expressed their unholy delight in the certainty of our destruction by the enemy.

By the time my regiment had reached the plateau night had put an end to the struggle. A sputter of rifles would break out now and then, followed perhaps by a spiritless hurrah. Occasionally a shell from a far-away battery would come pitching down somewhere near, with a whir crescendo, or flit above our heads with a whisper like that made by the wings of a night bird, to smother itself in the river. But there was no more fighting. The gunboats, however, blazed away at set intervals all night long, just to make the enemy uncomfortable and break him of his rest.

For us there was no rest. Foot by foot we moved through the dusky fields, we knew not whither. There were men all about us, but no camp-fires; to have made a blaze would have been madness. The men were of strange regiments; they mentioned the names of unknown generals. They gathered in groups by the wayside, asking eagerly our numbers. They recounted the depressing incidents of the day. A thoughtful officer shut their mouths with a sharp word as he passed; a wise one coming after encouraged them to repeat their doleful tale all along the line.

Hidden in hollows and behind clumps of rank brambles were large tents, dimly lighted with candles, but looking comfortable. The kind of comfort they supplied was indicated by pairs of men entering and reappearing, bearing litters; by low moans from within and by long rows of dead with covered faces outside. These tents were constantly receiving the wounded, yet were never full; they were continually ejecting the dead, yet were never empty. It was as if the helpless had been carried in and murdered, that they might not hamper those whose business it was to fall to-morrow.

The night was now black-dark; as is usual after a battle, it had begun to rain. Still we moved; we were being put into position by somebody. Inch by inch we crept along, treading on one another's heels by way of keeping together. Commands were passed along the line in whispers; more commonly none were given. When the men had pressed so closely together that they could advance no farther they stood stock-still, sheltering the locks of their rifles with their ponchos. In this position many fell asleep. When those in front suddenly stepped away those in the rear, roused by the tramping, hastened after with such zeal that the line was soon choked again. Evidently the head of the division was being piloted at a snail's pace by some one who did not feel sure of his ground. Very often we struck our feet against the dead; more frequently against those who still had spirit enough to resent it with a moan. These were lifted carefully to one side and abandoned. Some had sense enough to ask in their weak way for water. Absurd! Their clothes were soaken, their hair dank; their white faces, dimly discernible, were clammy and cold. Besides, none of us had any water. There was plenty coming, though, for before midnight a thunderstorm broke upon us with great violence. The rain, which had for hours been a dull drizzle, fell with a copiousness that stifled us; we moved in running water up to our ankles. Happily, we were in a forest of great trees heavily "decorated" with Spanish moss, or with an enemy standing to his guns the disclosures of the lightning might have been inconvenient. As it was, the incessant blaze enabled us to consult our watches and encouraged us by displaying our numbers; our black, sinuous line, creeping like a giant serpent beneath the trees, was apparently interminable. I am almost ashamed to say how sweet I found the companionship of those coarse men.

So the long night wore away, and as the glimmer of morning crept in through the forest we found ourselves in a more open country. But where? Not a sign of battle was here. The trees were neither splintered nor scarred, the underbrush was unmown, the ground had no footprints but our own. It was as if we had broken into glades sacred to eternal silence. I should not have been surprised to see sleek leopards come fawning about our feet, and milk-white deer confront us with human eyes.

A few inaudible commands from an invisible leader had placed us in order of battle. But where was the enemy? Where, too, were the riddled regiments that we had come to save? Had our other divisions arrived during the night and passed the river to assist us? or were we to oppose our paltry five thousand breasts to an army flushed with victory? What protected our right? Who lay upon our left? Was there really anything in our front?

There came, borne to us on the raw morning air, the long, weird note of a bugle. It was directly before us. It rose with a low, clear, deliberate warble, and seemed to float in the gray sky like the note of a lark. The bugle calls of the Federal and the Confederate armies were the same: it was the "assembly"! As it died away I observed that the atmosphere had suffered a change; despite the equilibrium established by the storm, it was electric. Wings were growing on blistered feet. Bruised muscles and jolted bones, shoulders pounded

by the cruel knapsack, eyelids leaden from lack of sleep—
all were pervaded by the subtle fluid, all were unconscious
of their clay. The men thrust forward their heads, expanded
their eyes and clenched their teeth. They breathed hard, as if
throttled by tugging at the leash. If you had laid your hand in
the beard or hair of one of these men it would have crackled
and shot sparks.

VI

I suppose the country lying between Corinth and Pittsburg Landing could boast a few inhabitants other than alligators. What manner of people they were it is impossible to say, inasmuch as the fighting dispersed, or possibly exterminated them; perhaps in merely classing them as non-saurian I shall describe them with sufficient particularity and at the same time avert from myself the natural suspicion attaching to a writer who points out to persons who do not know him the peculiarities of persons whom he does not know. One thing, however, I hope I may without offense affirm of these swamp-dwellers—they were pious. To what deity their veneration was given—whether, like the Egyptians, they worshiped the crocodile, or, like other Americans, adored themselves, I do not presume to guess. But whoever, or whatever, may have been the divinity whose ends they shaped, unto Him, or It, they had builded a temple. This humble edifice, centrally situated in the heart of a solitude, and conveniently accessible to the supersylvan crow, had been christened Shiloh Chapel, whence the name of the battle. The fact of a Christian church—assuming it to have been a Christian church—giving name to a wholesale cutting of Christian throats by Christian hands need not be dwelt on here; the frequency of its recurrence in the history of our species has somewhat abated the moral interest that would otherwise attach to it.

VII

Owing to the darkness, the storm and the absence of a road, it had been impossible to move the artillery from the open ground about the Landing. The privation was much greater in a moral than in a material sense. The infantry soldier feels a confidence in this cumbrous arm quite unwarranted by its actual achievements in thinning out the opposition. There is something that inspires confidence in the way a gun dashes up to the front, shoving fifty or a hundred men to one side as if it said, " Permit me!" Then it squares its shoulders, calmly dislocates a joint in its back, sends away its twenty-four legs and settles down with a quiet rattle which says as plainly as possible, "I've come to stay." There is a superb scorn in its grimly defiant attitude, with its nose in the air; it appears not so much to threaten the enemy as deride him.

Our batteries were probably toiling after us somewhere; we could only hope the enemy might delay his attack until they should arrive. "He may delay his defense if he like," said a sententious young officer to whom I had imparted this natural wish. He had read the signs aright; the words were hardly spoken when a group of staff officers about the brigade commander shot away in divergent lines as if scattered by a whirlwind, and galloping each to the commander of a regiment gave the word. There was a momentary confusion of tongues, a thin line of skirmishers detached itself from the compact front and pushed forward, followed by its diminutive reserves of half a company each—one of which platoons it was my fortune to command. When the straggling line of skirmishers had swept four or five hundred yards ahead, "See," said one of my comrades, "she moves!" She did indeed, and in fine style, her front as straight as a string, her reserve regiments in columns doubled on the center, following in true subordination; no braying of brass to apprise the enemy, no fifing and drumming to amuse him; no ostentation of gaudy flags; no nonsense. This was a matter of business.

In a few moments we had passed out of the singular oasis that had so marvelously escaped the desolation of battle, and now the evidences of the previous day's struggle were present in profusion. The ground was tolerably level here, the forest less dense, mostly clear of undergrowth, and occasionally opening out into small natural meadows. Here and there were small pools—mere discs of rainwater with a tinge of blood. Riven and torn with cannon-shot, the trunks of the trees protruded bunches of splinters like hands, the fingers above the wound interlacing with those below. Large branches had been lopped, and hung their green heads to the ground, or swung critically in their netting of vines, as in a hammock. Many had been cut clean off and their masses of foliage seriously impeded the progress of the troops. The bark of these trees, from the root upward to a height of ten or twenty feet, was so thickly pierced with bullets and grape that one could not have laid a hand on it without covering several punctures. None had escaped. How the human body survives a storm like this must be explained by the fact that it is exposed to it but a few moments at a time, whereas these grand old trees had had no one to take their places, from the rising to the going down of the sun. Angular bits of iron, concavo-convex, sticking in the sides of muddy depressions, showed where shells had exploded in their furrows. Knapsacks, canteens, haversacks distended with soaken and swollen biscuits, gaping to disgorge, blankets beaten into the soil by the rain, rifles with bent barrels or splintered stocks, waist-belts, hats and the omnipresent sardine-box—all the wretched debris of the battle still littered the spongy earth as far as one could see, in every direction. Dead horses were everywhere; a few disabled caissons, or limbers, reclining on one elbow, as it were; ammunition wagons standing disconsolate behind four or six sprawling mules. Men? There were men enough; all dead, apparently, except one, who lay near where I had halted my platoon to await the slower movement of the line—a Federal sergeant, variously hurt, who had been a fine giant in his time. He lay face upward, taking in his breath in convulsive, rattling snorts, and blowing it out in sputters of froth which crawled creamily down his cheeks, piling itself alongside his neck and ears. A bullet had clipped a groove in his skull, above the temple; from this the brain protruded in bosses, dropping off in flakes and strings. I had not previously known one could get on, even in this unsatisfactory fashion, with so little brain. One of my men, whom I knew for a womanish fellow, asked if he should put his bayonet through him. Inexpressibly shocked by the cold-blooded proposal, I told him I thought not; it was unusual, and too many were looking.

VIII

It was plain that the enemy had retreated to Corinth. The arrival of our fresh troops and their successful passage of the river had disheartened him. Three or four of his gray cavalry videttes moving amongst the trees on the crest of a hill in our front, and galloping out of sight at the crack of our skirmishers' rifles, confirmed us in the belief; an army face to face with its enemy does not employ cavalry to watch its front. True, they might be a general and his staff. Crowning this rise we found a level field, a quarter of a mile in width; beyond it a gentle acclivity, covered with an undergrowth of young oaks, impervious to sight. We pushed on into the open, but the division halted at the edge. Having orders to conform to its movements, we halted too; but that did not suit; we received an intimation to proceed. I had performed this sort of service before, and in the exercise of my discretion deployed my platoon, pushing it forward at a run, with trailed arms, to strengthen the skirmish line, which I overtook some thirty or forty yards from the wood. Then—I can't describe it—the forest seemed all at once to flame up and disappear with a crash like that of a great wave upon the beach—a crash that expired in hot hissings, and the sickening "spat" of lead against flesh. A dozen of my brave fellows tumbled over like ten-pins. Some struggled to their feet, only to go down again, and yet again. Those who stood fired into the smoking brush and doggedly retired. We had expected to find, at most, a line of skirmishers similar to our own; it was with a view to overcoming them by a sudden coup at the moment of collision that I had thrown forward my little reserve. What we had found was a line of battle, coolly holding its fire till it could count our teeth. There was no more to be done but get back across the open ground, every superficial yard of which was throwing up its little jet of mud provoked by an impinging bullet. We got back, most of us, and I shall never forget the ludicrous incident of a young officer who had taken part in the affair walking up to his colonel, who had been a calm and apparently impartial spectator, and gravely reporting: "The enemy is in force just beyond this field, sir."

IX

In subordination to the design of this narrative, as defined by its title, the incidents related necessarily group themselves about my own personality as a center; and, as this center, during the few terrible hours of the engagement, maintained a variably constant relation to the open field already mentioned, it is important that the reader should bear in mind the topographical and tactical features of the local situation. The hither side of the field was occupied by the front of my brigade—a length of two regiments in line, with proper intervals for field batteries. During the entire fight the enemy held the slight wooded acclivity beyond. The debatable ground to the right and left of the open was broken and thickly wooded for miles, in some places quite inaccessible to artillery and at very few points offering opportunities for its successful employment. As a consequence of this the two sides of the field were soon studded thickly with confronting guns, which flamed away at one another with amazing zeal and rather startling effect. Of course, an infantry attack delivered from either side was not to be thought of when the covered flanks offered inducements so unquestionably superior; and I believe the riddled bodies of my poor skirmishers were the only ones left on this "neutral ground" that day. But there was a very pretty line of dead continually growing in our rear, and doubtless the enemy had at his back a similar encouragement.

The configuration of the ground offered us no protection.

By lying flat on our faces between the guns we were screened from view by a straggling row of brambles, which marked the course of an obsolete fence; but the enemy's grape was sharper than his eyes, and it was poor consolation to know that his gunners could not see what they were doing, so long as they did it. The shock of our own pieces nearly deafened us, but in the brief intervals we could hear the battle roaring and stammering in the dark reaches of the forest to the right and left, where our other divisions were dashing themselves again and again into the smoking jungle. What would we not have given to join them in their brave, hopeless task! But to lie inglorious beneath showers of shrapnel darting divergent from the unassailable sky—meekly to be blown out of life by level gusts of grape—to clench our teeth and shrink helpless before big shot pushing noisily through the consenting air— this was horrible! "Lie down, there!" a captain would shout, and then get up himself to see that his order was obeyed. "Captain, take cover, sir!" the lieutenant-colonel would shriek, pacing up and down in the most exposed position that he could find.

O those cursed guns!—not the enemy's, but our own. Had it not been for them, we might have died like men. They must be supported, forsooth, the feeble, boasting bullies! It was impossible to conceive that these pieces were doing the enemy as excellent a mischief as his were doing us; they seemed to raise their "cloud by day" solely to direct aright the streaming procession of Confederate missiles. They no longer inspired confidence, but begot apprehension; and it was with grim satisfaction that I saw the carriage of one and another smashed into matchwood by a whooping shot and bundled out of the line.

X

The dense forests wholly or partly in which were fought so many battles of the Civil War, lay upon the earth in each autumn a thick deposit of dead leaves and stems, the decay of which forms a soil of surprising depth and richness. In dry weather the upper stratum is as inflammable as tinder. A fire once kindled in it will spread with a slow, persistent advance as far as local conditions permit, leaving a bed of light ashes beneath which the less combustible accretions of previous years will smolder until extinguished by rains. In many of the engagements of the war the fallen leaves took fire and roasted the fallen men. At Shiloh, during the first day's fighting, wide tracts of woodland were burned over in this way and scores of wounded who might have recovered perished in slow torture. I remember a deep ravine a little to the left and rear of the field I have described, in which, by some mad freak of heroic incompetence, a part of an Illinois regiment had been surrounded, and refusing to surrender was destroyed, as it very well deserved. My regiment having at last been relieved at the guns and moved over to the heights above this ravine for no obvious purpose, I obtained leave to go down into the valley of death and gratify a reprehensible curiosity.

Forbidding enough it was in every way. The fire had swept every superficial foot of it, and at every step I sank into ashes to the ankle. It had contained a thick undergrowth of young saplings, every one of which had been severed by a bullet, the foliage of the prostrate tops being afterward burnt and the stumps charred. Death had put his sickle into this thicket and fire had gleaned the field. Along a line which was not that of extreme depression, but was at every point significantly equidistant from the heights on either hand, lay the bodies, half buried in ashes; some in the unlovely looseness of attitude denoting sudden death by the bullet, but by far the greater number in postures of agony that told of the tormenting flame. Their clothing was half burnt away— their hair and beard entirely; the rain had come too late to save their nails. Some were swollen to double girth; others shriveled to manikins. According to degree of exposure, their faces were bloated and black or yellow and shrunken. The contraction of muscles which had given them claws for hands had cursed each countenance with a hideous grin. Faugh! I cannot catalogue the charms of these gallant gentlemen who had got what they enlisted for.

XI

It was now three o'clock in the afternoon, and raining. For fifteen hours we had been wet to the skin. Chilled, sleepy, hungry and disappointed—profoundly disgusted with the inglorious part to which they had been condemned—the men of my regiment did everything doggedly. The spirit had gone quite out of them. Blue sheets of powder smoke, drifting amongst the trees, settling against the hillsides and beaten into nothingness by the falling rain, filled the air with their peculiar pungent odor, but it no longer stimulated. For miles on either hand could be heard the hoarse murmur of the battle, breaking out near by with frightful distinctness, or sinking to a murmur in the distance; and the one sound aroused no more attention than the other.

We had been placed again in rear of those guns, but even they and their iron antagonists seemed to have tired of their feud, pounding away at one another with amiable infrequency. The right of the regiment extended a little beyond the field. On the prolongation of the line in that direction were some regiments of another division, with one in reserve. A third of a mile back lay the remnant of somebody's brigade looking to its wounds. The line of forest bounding this end of the field stretched as straight as a wall from the right of my regiment to Heaven knows what regiment of the enemy. There suddenly appeared, marching down along this wall, not more than two hundred yards in our front, a dozen files of gray-clad men with rifles on the right shoulder. At an interval of fifty yards they were followed by perhaps half as many more; and in fair supporting distance of these stalked with confident mien a single man! There seemed to me something indescribably ludicrous in the advance of this handful of men upon an army, albeit with their left flank protected by a forest. It does not so impress me now. They were the exposed flanks of three lines of infantry, each half a mile in length. In a moment our gunners had grappled with the nearest pieces, swung them half round, and were pouring streams of canister into the invaded wood. The infantry rose in masses, springing into line. Our threatened regiments stood like a wall, their loaded rifles at "ready," their bayonets hanging quietly in the scabbards. The right wing of my own regiment was thrown slightly backward to threaten the flank of the assault. The battered brigade away to the rear pulled itself together.

Then the storm burst. A great gray cloud seemed to spring out of the forest into the faces of the waiting battalions. It was received with a crash that made the very trees turn up their leaves. For one instant the assailants paused above their dead, then struggled forward, their bayonets glittering in the eyes that shone behind the smoke. One moment, and those unmoved men in blue would be impaled. What were they about? Why did they not fix bayonets? Were they stunned by their own volley? Their inaction was maddening! Another tremendous crash!—the rear rank had fired! Humanity, thank Heaven! is not made for this, and the shattered gray mass drew back a score of paces, opening a feeble fire. Lead had scored its old-time victory over steel; the heroic had broken its great heart against the commonplace. There are those who say that it is sometimes otherwise.

All this had taken but a minute of time, and now the second Confederate line swept down and poured in its fire. The line of blue staggered and gave way; in those two terrific volleys it seemed to have quite poured out its spirit. To this deadly work our reserve regiment now came up with a run. It was surprising to see it spitting fire with never a sound, for such was the infernal din that the ear could take in no more. This fearful scene was enacted within fifty paces of our toes, but we were rooted to the ground as if we had grown there. But now our commanding officer rode from behind us to the front, waved his hand with the courteous gesture that says apres vous, and with a barely audible cheer we sprang into the fight. Again the smoking front of gray receded, and again, as the enemy's third line emerged from its leafy covert, it pushed forward across the piles of dead and wounded to threaten with protruded steel. Never was seen so striking a proof of the paramount importance of numbers. Within an area of three hundred yards by fifty there struggled for front places no fewer than six regiments; and the accession of each, after the first collision, had it not been immediately counterpoised, would have turned the scale.

As matters stood, we were now very evenly matched, and how long we might have held out God only knows. But all at once something appeared to have gone wrong with the enemy's left; our men had somewhere pierced his line. A moment later his whole front gave way, and springing forward with fixed bayonets we pushed him in utter confusion back to his original line. Here, among the tents from which Grant's people had been expelled the day before, our broken and disordered regiments inextricably intermingled, and drunken with the wine of triumph, dashed confidently against a pair of trim battalions, provoking a tempest of hissing lead that made us stagger under its very weight. The sharp onset of another against our flank sent us whirling back with fire at our heels and fresh foes in merciless pursuit—who in their turn were broken upon the front of the invalided brigade previously mentioned, which had moved up from the rear to assist in this lively work.

As we rallied to reform behind our beloved guns and noted the ridiculous brevity of our line—as we sank from sheer fatigue, and tried to moderate the terrific thumping of our hearts—as we caught our breath to ask who had seen such-and-such a comrade, and laughed hysterically at the reply—there swept past us and over us into the open field a long regiment with fixed bayonets and rifles on the right shoulder. Another followed, and another; two—three—four! Heavens! where do all these men come from, and why did they not come before? How grandly and confidently they go sweeping on like long blue waves of ocean chasing one another to the cruel rocks! Involuntarily we draw in our weary feet beneath us as we sit, ready to spring up and interpose our breasts when these gallant lines shall come back to us across the terrible field, and sift brokenly through among the trees with spouting fires at their backs. We still our breathing to catch the full grandeur of the volleys that are to tear them to shreds. Minute after minute passes and the sound does not come. Then for the first time we note that the silence of the whole region is not comparative, but absolute. Have we become stone deaf? See; here comes a stretcher-bearer, and there a surgeon! Good heavens! a chaplain!

The battle was indeed at an end.

XII

And this was, O so long ago! How they come back to me—dimly and brokenly, but with what a magic spell—those years of youth when I was soldiering! Again I hear the far warble of blown bugles. Again I see the tall, blue smoke of camp-fires ascending from the dim valleys of Wonderland. There steals upon my sense the ghost of an odor from pines that canopy the ambuscade. I feel upon my cheek the morning mist that shrouds the hostile camp unaware of its doom, and my blood stirs at the ringing rifle-shot of the solitary sentinel. Unfamiliar landscapes, glittering with sunshine or sullen with rain, come to me demanding recognition, pass, vanish and give place to others. Here in the night stretches a wide and blasted field studded with half-extinct fires burning redly with I know not what presage of evil. Again I shudder as I note its desolation and its awful silence. Where was it? To what monstrous inharmony of death was it the visible prelude?

O days when all the world was beautiful and strange; when unfamiliar constellations burned in the Southern midnights, and the mocking-bird poured out his heart in the moon-gilded magnolia; when there was something new under a new sun; will your fine, far memories ever cease to lay contrasting pictures athwart the harsher features of this later world, accentuating the ugliness of the longer and tamer life? Is it not strange that the phantoms of a blood-stained period have so airy a grace and look with so tender eyes?—that I recall with difficulty the danger and death and horrors of the time, and without effort all that was gracious and picturesque? Ah, Youth, there is no such wizard as thou! Give me but one touch of thine artist hand upon the dull canvas of the Present; gild for but one moment the drear and somber scenes of to-day, and I will willingly surrender an other life than the one that I should have thrown away at Shiloh.

Four Days in Dixie

First published in 1888.

During a part of the month of October, 1864, the Federal and Confederate armies of Sherman and Hood respectively, having performed a surprising and resultless series of marches and countermarches since the fall of Atlanta, confronted each other along the separating line of the Coosa River in the vicinity of Gaylesville, Alabama. Here for several days they remained at rest—at least most of the infantry and artillery did; what the cavalry was doing nobody but itself ever knew or greatly cared. It was an interregnum of expectancy between two régimes of activity.

I was on the staff of Colonel McConnell, who commanded an infantry brigade in the absence of its regular commander. McConnell was a good man, but he did not keep a very tight rein upon the half dozen restless and reckless young fellows who (for his sins) constituted his "military family." In most matters we followed the trend of our desires,] which commonly ran in the direction of adventure—it did not greatly matter what kind. In pursuance of this policy of escapades, one bright Sunday morning Lieutenant Cobb, an aide-de-camp, and I mounted and set out to "seek our fortunes," as the story books have it. Striking into a road of which we knew nothing except that it led toward the river, we followed it for a mile or such a matter, when we found our advance interrupted by a considerable creek, which we must ford or go back. We consulted a moment and then rode at it as hard as we could, possibly in the belief that a high momentum would act as it does in the instance of a skater passing over thin ice. Cobb was fortunate enough to get across comparatively dry, but his hapless companion was utterly submerged. The disaster was all the greater from my having on a resplendent new uniform, of which I had been pardonably vain. Ah, what a gorgeous new uniform it never was again!

A half-hour devoted to wringing my clothing and dry-charging my revolver, and we were away. A brisk canter of a half-hour under the arches of the trees brought us to the river, where it was our ill luck to find a boat and three soldiers of our brigade. These men had been for several hours concealed in the brush patiently watching the opposite bank in the amiable hope of getting a shot at some unwary Confederate, but had seen none. For a great distance up and down the stream on the other side, and for at least a mile back from it, extended cornfields. Beyond the cornfields, on slightly higher ground, was a thin forest, with breaks here and there in its continuity, denoting plantations, probably. No houses were in sight, and no camps. We knew that it was the enemy's ground, but whether his forces were disposed along the slightly higher country bordering the bottom lands, or at strategic points miles back, as ours were, we knew no more than the least curious private in our army. In any case the river line would naturally be picketed or patrolled. But the charm of the unknown was upon us: the mysterious exerted its old-time fascination, beckoning to us from that silent shore so peaceful and dreamy in the beauty of the quiet Sunday morning. The temptation was strong and we fell. The soldiers were as eager for the hazard as we, and readily volunteered for the madmen's enterprise. Concealing our horses in a cane-brake, we unmoored the boat and rowed across unmolested.

Arrived at a kind of "landing" on the other side, our first care was so to secure the boat under the bank as to favor a hasty re-embarking in case we should be so unfortunate as to incur the natural consequence of our act; then, following an old road through the ranks of standing corn, we moved in force upon the Confederate position, five strong, with an armament of three Springfield rifles and two Colt's revolvers. We had not the further advantage of music and banners. One thing favored the expedition, giving it an apparent assurance of success: it was well officered—an officer to each man and a half.

After marching about a mile we came into a neck of woods and crossed an intersecting road which showed no wheel-tracks, but was rich in hoof-prints. We observed them and kept right on about our business, whatever that may have been. A few hundred yards farther brought us to a plantation bordering our road upon the right. The fields, as was the Southern fashion at that period of the war, were uncultivated and overgrown with brambles. A large white house stood at some little distance from the road; we saw women and children and a few negroes there. On our left ran the thin forest, pervious to cavalry. Directly ahead an ascent in the road formed a crest beyond which we could see nothing.

On this crest suddenly appeared two horsemen in gray, sharply outlined against the sky—men and animals looking gigantic. At the same instant a jingling and tramping were audible behind us, and turning in that direction I saw a score of mounted men moving forward at a trot. In the meantime the giants on the crest had multiplied surprisingly. Our invasion of the Gulf States had apparently failed.

There was lively work in the next few seconds. The shots were thick and fast—and uncommonly loud; none, I think, from our side. Cobb was on the extreme left of our advance, I on the right—about two paces apart. He instantly dived into the wood. The three men and I climbed across the fence somehow and struck out across the field—actuated, doubtless, by an intelligent forethought: men on horseback could not immediately follow. Passing near the house, now swarming like a hive of bees, we made for a swamp two or three hundred yards away, where I concealed myself in a jungle, the others continuing—as a defeated commander would put it—to fall back. In my cover, where I lay panting like a hare, I could hear a deal of shouting and hard riding and an occasional shot. I heard some one calling dogs, and the thought of bloodhounds added its fine suggestiveness to the other fancies appropriate to the occasion.

Finding myself unpursued after the lapse of what seemed an hour, but was probably a few minutes, I cautiously sought a place where, still concealed, I could obtain a view of the field of glory. The only enemy in sight was a group of horsemen on a hill a quarter of a mile away. Toward this group a woman was running, followed by the eyes of everybody about the house. I thought she had discovered my hiding-place and was going to "give me away." Taking to my hands and knees I crept as rapidly as possible among the clumps of brambles directly back toward the point in the road where we had met the enemy and failed to make him ours. There I dragged myself into a patch of briars within ten feet of the road, where I lay undiscovered during the remainder of the day, listening to a variety of disparaging remarks upon Yankee valor and to dispiriting declarations of intention conditional on my capture, as members of the Opposition passed and repassed and paused in the road to discuss the morning's events. In this way I learned that the three privates had been headed off and caught within ten minutes. Their destination would naturally be Andersonville; what further became of them God knows. Their captors passed the day making a careful canvass of the swamp for me.

When night had fallen I cautiously left my place of concealment, dodged across the road into the woods and made for the river through the mile of corn. Such corn! It towered above me like a forest, shutting out all the starlight except what came from directly overhead. Many of the ears were a yard out of reach. One who has never seen an Alabama river-bottom cornfield has not exhausted nature's surprises; nor will he know what solitude is until he explores one in a moonless night.

I came at last to the river bank with its fringe of trees and willows and canes. My intention was to swim across, but the current was swift, the water forbiddingly dark and cold. A mist obscured the other bank. I could not, indeed, see the water more than a few yards out. It was a hazardous and horrible undertaking, and I gave it up, following cautiously along the bank in search of the spot where we had moored the boat. True, it was hardly likely that the landing was now unguarded, or, if so, that the boat was still there. Cobb had undoubtedly made for it, having an even more urgent need than I; but hope springs eternal in the human breast, and there was a chance that he had been killed before reaching it. I came at last into the road that we had taken and consumed half the night in cautiously approaching the landing, pistol in hand and heart in mouth. The boat was gone! I continued my journey along the stream—in search of another.

My clothing was still damp from my morning bath, my teeth rattled with cold, but I kept on along the stream until I reached the limit of the cornfields and entered a dense wood. Through this I groped my way, inch by inch, when, suddenly emerging from a thicket into a space slightly more open, I came upon a smoldering camp-fire surrounded by prostrate figures of men, upon one of whom I had almost trodden. A sentinel, who ought to have been shot, sat by the embers, his carbine across his lap, his chin upon his breast. Just beyond was a group of unsaddled horses. The men were asleep; the sentinel was asleep; the horses were asleep. There was something indescribably uncanny about it all. For a moment

I believed them all lifeless, and O'Hara's familiar line, "The bivouac of the dead," quoted itself in my consciousness. The emotion that I felt was that inspired by a sense of the supernatural; of the actual and imminent peril of my position I had no thought. When at last it occurred to me I felt it as a welcome relief, and stepping silently back into the shadow retraced my course without having awakened a soul. The vividness with which I can now recall that scene is to me one of the marvels of memory.

Getting my bearings again with some difficulty, I now made a wide detour to the left, in the hope of passing around this outpost and striking the river beyond. In this mad attempt I ran upon a more vigilant sentinel, posted in the heart of a thicket, who fired at me without challenge. To a soldier an unexpected shot ringing out at dead of night is fraught with an awful significance. In my circumstances— cut off from my comrades, groping about an unknown country, surrounded by invisible perils which such a signal would call into eager activity—the flash and shock of that firearm were unspeakably dreadful! In any case I should and ought to have fled, and did so; but how much or little of conscious prudence there was in the prompting I do not care to discover by analysis of memory. I went back into the corn, found the river, followed it back a long way and mounted into the fork of a low tree. There I perched until the dawn, a most uncomfortable bird.

In the gray light of the morning I discovered that I was opposite an island of considerable length, separated from the mainland by a narrow and shallow channel, which I promptly waded. The island was low and flat, covered with an almost impenetrable cane-brake interlaced with vines. Working my way through these to the other side, I obtained another look at God's country—Shermany, so to speak. There were no visible inhabitants. The forest and the water met. This did not deter me. For the chill of the water I had no further care, and laying off my boots and outer clothing I prepared to swim. A strange thing now occurred—more accurately, a familiar thing occurred at a strange moment. A black cloud seemed to pass before my eyes—the water, the trees, the sky, all vanished in a profound darkness. I heard the roaring of a great cataract, felt the earth sinking from beneath my feet. Then I heard and felt no more.

At the battle of Kennesaw Mountain in the previous June I had been badly wounded in the head, and for three months was incapacitated for service. In truth, I had done no actual duty since, being then, as for many years afterward, subject to fits of fainting, sometimes without assignable immediate cause, but mostly when suffering from exposure, excitement or excessive fatigue. This combination of them all had broken me down—most opportunely, it would seem.

When I regained my consciousness the sun was high. I was still giddy and half blind. To have taken to the water would have been madness; I must have a raft. Exploring my island, I found a pen of slender logs: an old structure without roof or rafters, built for what purpose I do not know. Several of these logs I managed with patient toil to detach and convey to the water, where I floated them, lashing them together with vines. Just before sunset my raft was complete and freighted with my outer clothing, boots and pistol. Having shipped the last article, I returned into the brake, seeking something from which to improvise a paddle. While peering about I heard a sharp metallic click—the cocking of a rifle! I was a prisoner.

The history of this great disaster to the Union arms is brief and simple. A Confederate "home guard," hearing something going on upon the island, rode across, concealed his horse and still-hunted me. And, reader, when you are "held up" in the same way may it be by as fine a fellow. He not only spared my life, but even overlooked a feeble and ungrateful after-attempt upon his own (the particulars of which I shall not relate), merely exacting my word of honor that I would not again try to escape while in his custody. Escape! I could not have escaped a new-born babe.

At my captor's house that evening there was a reception, attended by the élite of the whole vicinity. A Yankee officer in full fig—minus only the boots, which could not be got on to his swollen feet—was something worth seeing, and those who came to scoff remained to stare. What most interested them, I think, was my eating—an entertainment that was prolonged to a late hour. They were a trifle disappointed by the absence of horns, hoof and tail, but bore their chagrin with good-natured fortitude. Among my visitors was a charming young woman from the plantation where we had met the foe the day before—the same lady whom I had suspected of an intention to reveal my hiding-place. She had had no such design; she had run over to the group of horsemen to learn if her father had been hurt—by whom, I should like to know. No restraint was put upon me; my captor even left me with the women and children and went off for instructions as to what disposition he should make of me. Altogether the reception was "a pronounced success," though it is to be regretted that the guest of the evening had the incivility to fall dead asleep in the midst of the festivities, and was put to bed by sympathetic and, he has reason to believe, fair hands.

The next morning I was started off to the rear in custody of two mounted men, heavily armed. They had another prisoner, picked up in some raid beyond the river. He was a most offensive brute—a foreigner of some mongrel sort, with just sufficient command of our tongue to show that he could not control his own. We traveled all day, meeting occasional small bodies of cavalrymen, by whom, with one exception—a Texan officer—was civilly treated. My guards said, however, that if we should chance to meet Jeff Gatewood he would probably take me from them and hang me to the nearest tree; and once or twice, hearing horsemen approach, they directed me to stand aside, concealed in the brush, one of them remaining near by to keep an eye on me, the other going forward with my fellow-prisoner, for whose neck they seemed to have less tenderness, and whom I heartily wished well hanged.

Jeff Gatewood was a "guerrilla" chief of local notoriety, who was a greater terror to his friends than to his other foes.

My guards related almost incredible tales of his cruelties and infamies. By their account it was into his camp that I had blundered on Sunday night.

We put up for the night at a farmhouse, having gone not more than fifteen miles, owing to the condition of my feet. Here we got a bite of supper and were permitted to lie before the fire. My fellow-prisoner took off his boots and was soon sound asleep. I took off nothing and, despite exhaustion, remained equally sound awake. One of the guards also removed his footgear and outer clothing, placed his weapons under his neck and slept the sleep of innocence; the other sat in the chimney corner on watch. The house was a double log cabin, with an open space between the two parts, roofed over—a common type of habitation in that region. The room we were in had its entrance in this open space, the fireplace opposite, at the end. Beside the door was a bed, occupied by the old man of the house and his wife. It was partly curtained off from the room.

In an hour or two the chap on watch began to yawn, then to nod. Pretty soon he stretched himself on the floor, facing us, pistol in hand. For a while he supported himself on his elbow, then laid his head on his arm, blinking like an owl. I performed an occasional snore, watching him narrowly between my eyelashes from the shadow of my arm. The inevitable occurred—he slept audibly.

A half-hour later I rose quietly to my feet, particularly careful not to disturb the blackguard at my side, and moved as silently as possible to the door. Despite my care the latch clicked. The old lady sat bolt upright in bed and stared at me. She was too late. I sprang through the door and struck out for the nearest point of woods, in a direction previously selected, vaulting fences like an accomplished gymnast and followed by a multitude of dogs. It is said that the State of Alabama has more dogs than school-children, and that they cost more for their keep. The estimate of cost is probably too high.

Looking backward as I ran, I saw and heard the place in a turmoil and uproar; and to my joy the old man, evidently oblivious to the facts of the situation, was lifting up his voice and calling his dogs. They were good dogs: they went back; otherwise the malicious old rascal would have had my skeleton. Again the traditional bloodhound did not materialize. Other pursuit there was no reason to fear; my foreign gentleman would occupy the attention of one of the soldiers, and in the darkness of the forest I could easily elude the other, or, if need be, get him at a disadvantage. In point of fact there was no pursuit.

I now took my course by the north star (which I can never sufficiently bless), avoiding all roads and open places about houses, laboriously boring my way through forests, driving myself like a wedge into brush and bramble, swimming every stream I came to (some of them more than once, probably), and pulling myself out of the water by boughs and briars—whatever could be grasped. Let any one try to go a little way across even the most familiar country on a moonless night, and he will have an experience to remember. By dawn I had probably not made three miles. My clothing and skin were alike in rags.

During the day I was compelled to make wide detours to avoid even the fields, unless they were of corn; but in other respects the going was distinctly better. A light breakfast of raw sweet potatoes and persimmons cheered the inner man; a good part of the outer was decorating the several thorns, boughs and sharp rocks along my sylvan wake.

Late in the afternoon I found the river, at what point it was impossible to say. After a half-hour's rest, concluding with a fervent prayer that I might go to the bottom, I swam across. Creeping up the bank and holding my course still northward through a dense undergrowth, I suddenly reeled into a dusty highway and saw a more heavenly vision than ever the eyes of a dying saint were blessed withal—two patriots in blue carrying a stolen pig slung upon a pole!

Late that evening Colonel McConnell and his staff were chatting by a camp-fire in front of his headquarters. They were in a pleasant humor: some one had just finished a funny story about a man cut in two by a cannon-shot. Suddenly something staggered in among them from the outer darkness and fell into the fire. Somebody dragged it out by what seemed to be a leg. They turned the animal on its back and examined it—they were no cowards.

"What is it, Cobb?" said the chief, who had not taken the trouble to rise.

"I don't know, Colonel, but thank God it is dead!"

It was not.

The Crime at Pickett's Mill

First published in 1888.

There is a class of events which by their very nature, and despite any intrinsic interest that they may possess, are foredoomed to oblivion. They are merged in the general story of those greater events of which they were a part, as the thunder of a billow breaking on a distant beach is unnoted in the continuous roar. To how many having knowledge of the battles of our Civil War does the name Pickett's Mill suggest acts of heroism and devotion performed in scenes of awful carnage to accomplish the impossible? Buried in the official reports of the victors there are indeed imperfect accounts of the engagement: the vanquished have not thought it expedient to relate it. It is ignored by General Sherman in his memoirs, yet Sherman ordered it. General Howard wrote an account of the campaign of which it was an incident, and dismissed it in a single sentence; yet General Howard planned it, and it was fought as an isolated and independent action under his eye. Whether it was so trifling an affair as to justify this inattention let the reader judge.

The fight occurred on the 27th of May, 1864, while the armies of Generals Sherman and Johnston confronted each other near Dallas, Georgia, during the memorable "Atlanta campaign." For three weeks we had been pushing the Confederates southward, partly by manoeuvring, partly by fighting, out of Dalton, out of Resaca, through Adairsville,

Kingston and Cassville. Each army offered battle everywhere, but would accept it only on its own terms. At Dallas Johnston made another stand and Sherman, facing the hostile line, began his customary manoeuvring for an advantage. General Wood's division of Howard's corps occupied a position opposite the Confederate right. Johnston finding himself on the 26th overlapped by Schofield, still farther to Wood's left, retired his right (Polk) across a creek, whither we followed him into the woods with a deal of desultory bickering, and at nightfall had established the new lines at nearly a right angle with the old—Schofield reaching well around and threatening the Confederate rear.

The civilian reader must not suppose when he reads accounts of military operations in which relative positions of the forces are defined, as in the foregoing passages, that these were matters of general knowledge to those engaged. Such statements are commonly made, even by those high in command, in the light of later disclosures, such as the enemy's official reports. It is seldom, indeed, that a subordinate officer knows anything about the disposition of the enemy's forces—except that it is unaimable—or precisely whom he is fighting. As to the rank and file, they can know nothing more of the matter than the arms they carry. They hardly know what troops are upon their own right or left the length of a regiment away. If it is a cloudy day they are ignorant even of the points of the compass. It may be said, generally, that a soldier's knowledge of what is going on about him is coterminous with his official relation to it and his personal connection with it; what is going on in front of him he does not know at all until he learns it afterward.

At nine o'clock on the morning of the 27th Wood's division was withdrawn and replaced by Stanley's. Supported by Johnson's division, it moved at ten o'clock to the left, in the rear of Schofield, a distance of four miles through a forest, and at two o'clock in the afternoon had reached a position where General Howard believed himself free to move in behind the enemy's forces and attack them in the rear, or at least, striking them in the flank, crush his way along their line in the direction of its length, throw them into confusion and prepare an easy victory for a supporting attack in front. In selecting General Howard for this bold adventure General Sherman was doubtless not unmindful of Chancellorsville, where Stonewall Jackson had executed a similar manoeuvre for Howard's instruction. Experience is a normal school: it teaches how to teach.

There are some differences to be noted. At Chancellorsville it was Jackson who attacked; at Pickett's Mill, Howard. At Chancellorsville it was Howard who was assailed; at Pickett's Mill, Hood. The significance of the first distinction is doubled by that of the second.

The attack, it was understood, was to be made in column of brigades, Hazen's brigade of Wood's division leading. That such was at least Hazen's understanding I learned from his own lips during the movement, as I was an officer of his staff. But after a march of less than a mile an hour and a further delay of three hours at the end of it to acquaint the enemy of our intention to surprise him, our single shrunken brigade of fifteen hundred men was sent forward without support to double up the army of General Johnston. "We will put in Hazen and see what success he has." In these words of General Wood to General Howard we were first apprised of the true nature of the distinction about to be conferred upon us.

General W.B. Hazen, a born fighter, an educated soldier, after the war Chief Signal Officer of the Army and now long dead, was the best hated man that I ever knew, and his very memory is a terror to every unworthy soul in the service. His was a stormy life: he was in trouble all round. Grant, Sherman, Sheridan and a countless multitude of the less eminent luckless had the misfortune, at one time and another, to incur his disfavor, and he tried to punish them all. He was always—after the war—the central figure of a court-martial or a Congressional inquiry, was accused of everything, from stealing to cowardice, was banished to obscure posts, "jumped on" by the press, traduced in public and in private, and always emerged triumphant. While Signal Officer, he went up against the Secretary of War and put him to the controversial sword. He convicted Sheridan of falsehood, Sherman of barbarism, Grant of inefficiency. He was aggressive, arrogant, tyrannical, honorable, truthful, courageous—skillful soldier, a faithful friend and one of the most exasperating of men Duty was his religion, and like the Moslem he proselyted with the sword. His missionary efforts were directed chiefly against the spiritual darkness of his superiors in rank, though he would turn aside from pursuit of his erring commander to set a chicken-thieving orderly astride a wooden horse, with a heavy stone attached to each foot. "Hazen," said a brother brigadier, "is a synonym of insubordination." For my commander and my friend, my master in the art of war, now unable to answer for himself, let this fact answer: when he heard Wood say they would put him in and see what success he would have in defeating an army—when he saw Howard assent—he uttered never a word, rode to the head of his feeble brigade and patiently awaited the command to go. Only by a look which I knew how to read did he betray his sense of the criminal blunder.

The enemy had now had seven hours in which to learn of the movement and prepare to meet it. General Johnston says:

"The Federal troops extended their intrenched line [we did not intrench] so rapidly to their left that it was found necessary to transfer Cleburne's division to Hardee's corps to our right, where it was formed on the prolongation of Polk's line."

General Hood, commanding the enemy's right corps, says:

"On the morning of the 27th the enemy were known to be rapidly extending their left, attempting to turn my right as they extended. Cleburne was deployed to meet them, and at half-past five P.M. a very stubborn attack was made on this division, extending to the right, where Major-General Wheeler with his cavalry division was engaging them. The assault was continued with great determination upon both Cleburne and Wheeler."

That, then, was the situation: a weak brigade of fifteen hundred men, with masses of idle troops behind in the character of audience, waiting for the word to march a quarter-mile up hill through almost impassable tangles of underwood, along and across precipitous ravines, and attack breastworks constructed at leisure and manned with two divisions of troops as good as themselves. True, we did not know all this, but if any man on that ground besides Wood and Howard expected a "walkover" his must have been a singularly hopeful disposition. As topographical engineer it had been my duty to make a hasty examination of the ground in front. In doing so I had pushed far enough forward through the forest to hear distinctly the murmur of the enemy awaiting us, and this had been duly reported; but from our lines nothing could be heard but the wind among the trees and the songs of birds. Some one said it was a pity to frighten them, but there would necessarily be more or less noise. We laughed at that: men awaiting death on the battlefield laugh easily, though not infectiously.

The brigade was formed in four battalions, two in front and two in rear. This gave us a front of about two hundred yards. The right front battalion was commanded by Colonel R.L. Kimberly of the 41st Ohio, the left by Colonel O.H. Payne of the 124th Ohio, the rear battalions by Colonel J.C. Foy, 23d Kentucky, and Colonel W.W. Berry, 5th Kentucky— all brave and skillful officers, tested by experience on many fields. The whole command (known as the Second Brigade, Third Division, Fourth Corps) consisted of no fewer than nine regiments, reduced by long service to an average of less than two hundred men each. With full ranks and only the necessary details for special duty we should have had some eight thousand rifles in line.

We moved forward. In less than one minute the trim battalions had become simply a swarm of men struggling through the undergrowth of the forest, pushing and crowding. The front was irregularly serrated, the strongest and bravest in advance, the others following in fan-like formations, variable and inconstant, ever defining themselves anew. For the first two hundred yards our course lay along the left bank of a small creek in a deep ravine, our left battalions sweeping along its steep slope. Then we came to the fork of the ravine. A part of us crossed below, the rest above, passing over both branches, the regiments inextricably intermingled, rendering all military formation impossible. The color-bearers kept well to the front with their flags, closely furled, aslant backward over their shoulders. Displayed, they would have been torn to rags by the boughs of the trees. Horses were all sent to the rear; the general and staff and all the field officers toiled along on foot as best they could. "We shall halt and form when we get out of this," said an aide-de-camp.

Suddenly there were a ringing rattle of musketry, the familiar hissing of bullets, and before us the interspaces of the forest were all blue with smoke. Hoarse, fierce yells broke out of a thousand throats. The forward fringe of brave and hardy assailants was arrested in its mutable extensions; the edge of our swarm grew dense and clearly defined as the foremost halted, and the rest pressed forward to align themselves beside them, all firing. The uproar was deafening; the air was sibilant with streams and sheets of missiles. In the steady, unvarying roar of small-arms the frequent shock of the cannon was rather felt than heard, but the gusts of grape which they blew into that populous wood were audible enough, screaming among the trees and cracking against their stems and branches. We had, of course, no artillery to reply.

Our brave color-bearers were now all in the forefront of battle in the open, for the enemy had cleared a space in front of his breastworks. They held the colors erect, shook out their glories, waved them forward and back to keep them spread, for there was no wind. From where I stood, at the right of the line—we had "halted and formed," indeed—I could see six of our flags at one time. Occasionally one would go down, only to be instantly lifted by other hands.

I must here quote again from General Johnston's account of this engagement, for nothing could more truly indicate the resolute nature of the attack than the Confederate belief that it was made by the whole Fourth Corps, instead of one weak brigade:

"The Fourth Corps came on in deep order and assailed the Texans with great vigor, receiving their close and accurate fire with the fortitude always exhibited by General Sherman's troops in the actions of this campaign.... The Federal troops approached within a few yards of the Confederates, but at last were forced to give way by their storm of well-directed bullets, and fell back to the shelter of a hollow near and behind them. They left hundreds of corpses within twenty paces of the Confederate line. When the United States troops paused in their advance within fifteen paces of the Texan front rank one of their color-bearers planted his colors eight or ten feet in front of his regiment, and was instantly shot dead. A soldier sprang forward to his place and fell also as he grasped the color-staff. A second and third followed successively, and each received death as speedily as his predecessors. A fourth, however, seized and bore back the object of soldierly devotion."

Such incidents have occurred in battle from time to time since men began to venerate the symbols of their cause, but they are not commonly related by the enemy. If General Johnston had known that his veteran divisions were throwing their successive lines against fewer than fifteen hundred men his glowing tribute to his enemy's valor could hardly have been more generously expressed. I can attest the truth of his soldierly praise: I saw the occurrence that he relates and regret that I am unable to recall even the name of the regiment whose colors were so gallantly saved.

Early in my military experience I used to ask myself how it was that brave troops could retreat while still their courage was high. As long as a man is not disabled he can go forward; can it be anything but fear that makes him stop and finally retire? Are there signs by which he can infallibly know the struggle to be hopeless? In this engagement, as in others, my doubts were answered as to the fact; the explanation is still obscure. In many instances which have come under my observation, when hostile lines of infantry engage at close range and the assailants afterward retire, there was a "dead-line" beyond which no man advanced but to fall. Not a soul of them ever reached the enemy's front to be bayoneted or captured. It was a matter of the difference of three or four paces—too small a distance to affect the accuracy of aim. In these affairs no aim is taken at individual antagonists; the soldier delivers his fire at the thickest mass in his front. The fire is, of course, as deadly at twenty paces as at fifteen; at fifteen as at ten. Nevertheless, there is the "dead-line," with its well-defined edge of corpses—those of the bravest. Where both lines are fighting without cover—as in a charge met by a counter-charge—each has its "dead-line," and between the two is a clear space—neutral ground, devoid of dead, for the living cannot reach it to fall there.

I observed this phenomenon at Pickett's Mill. Standing at the right of the line I had an unobstructed view of the narrow, open space across which the two lines fought. It was dim with smoke, but not greatly obscured: the smoke rose and spread in sheets among the branches of the trees. Most of our men fought kneeling as they fired, many of them behind trees, stones and whatever cover they could get, but there were considerable groups that stood. Occasionally one of these groups, which had endured the storm of missiles for moments without perceptible reduction, would push forward, moved by a common despair, and wholly detach itself from the line. In a second every man of the group would be down. There had been no visible movement of the enemy, no audible change in the awful, even roar of the firing—yet all were down. Frequently the dim figure of an individual soldier would be seen to spring away from his comrades, advancing alone toward that fateful interspace, with leveled bayonet. He got no farther than the farthest of his predecessors. Of the "hundreds of corpses within twenty paces of the Confederate line," I venture to say that a third were within fifteen paces, and not one within ten.

It is the perception—perhaps unconscious—of this inexplicable phenomenon that causes the still unharmed, still vigorous and still courageous soldier to retire without having come into actual contact with his foe. He sees, or feels, that he cannot. His bayonet is a useless weapon for slaughter; its purpose is a moral one. Its mandate exhausted, he sheathes it and trusts to the bullet. That failing, he retreats. He has done all that he could do with such appliances as he has.

No command to fall back was given, none could have been heard. Man by man, the survivors withdrew at will, sifting through the trees into the cover of the ravines, among the wounded who could drag themselves back; among the skulkers whom nothing could have dragged forward. The left of our short line had fought at the corner of a cornfield, the fence along the right side of which was parallel to the direction of our retreat. As the disorganized groups fell back along this fence on the wooded side, they were attacked by a flanking force of the enemy moving through the field in a direction nearly parallel with what had been our front. This force, I infer from General Johnston's account, consisted of the brigade of General Lowry, or two Arkansas regiments under Colonel Baucum. I had been sent by General Hazen to that point and arrived in time to witness this formidable movement. But already our retreating men, in obedience to their officers, their courage and their instinct of self-preservation, had formed along the fence and opened fire. The apparently slight advantage of the imperfect cover and the open range worked its customary miracle: the assault, a singularly spiritless one, considering the advantages it promised and that it was made by an organized and victorious force against a broken and retreating one, was checked. The assailants actually retired, and if they afterward renewed the movement they encountered none but our dead and wounded.

The battle, as a battle, was at an end, but there was still some slaughtering that it was possible to incur before nightfall; and as the wreck of our brigade drifted back through the forest we met the brigade (Gibson's) which, had the attack been made in column, as it should have been, would have been but five minutes behind our heels, with another five minutes behind its own. As it was, just forty-five minutes had elapsed, during which the enemy had destroyed us and was now ready to perform the same kindly office for our successors. Neither Gibson nor the brigade which was sent to his "relief" as tardily as he to ours accomplished, or could have hoped to accomplish, anything whatever. I did not note their movements, having other duties, but Hazen in his "Narrative of Military Service" says:

"I witnessed the attack of the two brigades following my own, and none of these (troops) advanced nearer than one hundred yards of the enemy's works. They went in at a run, and as organizations were broken in less than a minute."

Nevertheless their losses were considerable, including several hundred prisoners taken from a sheltered place whence they did not care to rise and run. The entire loss was about fourteen hundred men, of whom nearly one-half fell killed and wounded in Hazen's brigade in less than thirty minutes of actual fighting.

General Johnston says:

"The Federal dead lying near our line were counted by many persons, officers and soldiers. According to these counts there were seven hundred of them."

This is obviously erroneous, though I have not the means at hand to ascertain the true number. I remember that we were all astonished at the uncommonly large proportion of dead to wounded—a consequence of the uncommonly close range at which most of the fighting was done.

The action took its name from a water-power mill near by. This was on a branch of a stream having, I am sorry to say, the prosaic name of Pumpkin Vine Creek. I have my own reasons for suggesting that the name of that water-course be altered to Sunday-School Run.

A Little of Chickamauga

First published in 1898.

The history of that awful struggle is well known—I have not the intention to record it here, but only to relate some part of what I saw of it; my purpose not instruction, but entertainment.

I was an officer of the staff of a Federal brigade. Chickamauga was not my first battle by many, for although hardly more than a boy in years, I had served at the front from the beginning of the trouble, and had seen enough of war to give me a fair understanding of it. We knew well enough that there was to be a fight: the fact that we did not want one would have told us that, for Bragg always retired when we wanted to fight and fought when we most desired peace. We had manoeuvred him out of Chattanooga, but had not manoeuvred our entire army into it, and he fell back so sullenly that those of us who followed, keeping him actually in sight, were a good deal more concerned about effecting a junction with the rest of our army than to push the pursuit. By the time that Rosecrans had got his three scattered corps together we were a long way from Chattanooga, with our line of communication with it so exposed that Bragg turned to seize it. Chickamauga was a fight for possession of a road.

Back along this road raced Crittenden's corps, with those of Thomas and McCook, which had not before traversed it. The whole army was moving by its left.

There was sharp fighting all along and all day, for the forest was so dense that the hostile lines came almost into contact before fighting was possible. One instance was particularly horrible. After some hours of close engagement my brigade, with foul pieces and exhausted cartridge boxes, was relieved and withdrawn to the road to protect several batteries of artillery—probably two dozen pieces—which commanded an open field in the rear of our line. Before our weary and virtually disarmed men had actually reached the guns the line in front gave way, fell back behind the guns and went on, the Lord knows whither. A moment later the field was gray with Confederates in pursuit. Then the guns opened fire with grape and canister and for perhaps five minutes—it seemed an hour—nothing could be heard but the infernal din of their discharge and nothing seen through the smoke but a great ascension of dust from the smitten soil. When all was over, and the dust cloud had lifted, the spectacle was too dreadful to describe. The Confederates were still there—all of them, it seemed—some almost under the muzzles of the guns. But not a man of all these brave fellows was on his feet, and so thickly were all covered with dust that they looked as if they had been reclothed in yellow.

"We bury our dead," said a gunner, grimly, though doubtless all were afterward dug out, for some were partly alive.

To a "day of danger" succeeded a "night of waking." The enemy, everywhere held back from the road, continued to stretch his line northward in the hope to overlap us and put himself between us and Chattanooga. We neither saw nor heard his movement, but any man with half a head would have known that he was making it, and we met it by a parallel movement to our left. By morning we had edged along a good way and thrown up rude intrenchments at a little distance from the road, on the threatened side. The day was not very far advanced when we were attacked furiously all along the line, beginning at the left. When repulsed, the enemy came again and again—his persistence was dispiriting. He seemed to be using against us the law of probabilities: of so many efforts one would eventually succeed.

One did, and it was my luck to see it win. I had been sent by my chief, General Hazen, to order up some artillery ammunition and rode away to the right and rear in search of it. Finding an ordnance train I obtained from the officer in charge a few wagons loaded with what I wanted, but he seemed in doubt as to our occupancy of the region across which I proposed to guide them. Although assured that I had just traversed it, and that it lay immediately behind Wood's division, he insisted on riding to the top of the ridge behind which his train lay and overlooking the ground. We did so, when to my astonishment I saw the entire country in front swarming with Confederates; the very earth seemed to be moving toward us! They came on in thousands, and so rapidly that we had barely time to turn tail and gallop down the hill and away, leaving them in possession of the train, many of the wagons being upset by frantic efforts to put them about. By what miracle that officer had sensed the situation I did not learn, for we parted company then and there and I never again saw him.

By a misunderstanding Wood's division had been withdrawn from our line of battle just as the enemy was making an assault. Through the gap of half a mile the Confederates charged without opposition, cutting our army clean in two. The right divisions were broken up and with General Rosecrans in their midst fled how they could across the country, eventually bringing up in Chattanooga, whence Rosecrans telegraphed to Washington the destruction of the rest of his army. The rest of his army was standing its ground.

A good deal of nonsense used to be talked about the heroism of General Garfield, who, caught in the rout of the right, nevertheless went back and joined the undefeated left under General Thomas. There was no great heroism in it; that is what every man should have done, including the commander of the army. We could hear Thomas's guns going—those of us who had ears for them—and all that was needful was to make a sufficiently wide detour and then move toward the sound. I did so myself, and have never felt that it ought to make me President. Moreover, on my way I met General Negley, and my duties as topographical engineer having given me some knowledge of the lay of the land offered to pilot him back to glory or the grave. I am sorry to say my good offices were rejected a little uncivilly, which I charitably attributed to the general's obvious absence of mind. His mind, I think, was in Nashville, behind a breastwork.

Unable to find my brigade, I reported to General Thomas,

who directed me to remain with him. He had assumed command of all the forces still intact and was pretty closely beset. The battle was fierce and continuous, the enemy extending his lines farther and farther around our right, toward our line of retreat. We could not meet the extension otherwise than by "refusing" our right flank and letting him inclose us; which but for gallant Gordon Granger he would inevitably have done.

This was the way of it. Looking across the fields in our rear (rather longingly) I had the happy distinction of a discoverer. What I saw was the shimmer of sunlight on metal: lines of troops were coming in behind us! The distance was too great, the atmosphere too hazy to distinguish the color of their uniform, even with a glass. Reporting my momentous "find" I was directed by the general to go and see who they were. Galloping toward them until near enough to see that they were of our kidney I hastened back with the glad tidings and was sent again, to guide them to the general's position.

It was General Granger with two strong brigades of the reserve, moving soldier-like toward the sound of heavy firing. Meeting him and his staff I directed him to Thomas, and unable to think of anything better to do decided to go visiting. I knew I had a brother in that gang—an officer of an Ohio battery. I soon found him near the head of a column, and as we moved forward we had a comfortable chat amongst such of the enemy's bullets as had inconsiderately been fired too high. The incident was a trifle marred by one of them unhorsing another officer of the battery, whom we propped against a tree and left. A few moments later Granger's force was put in on the right and the fighting was terrific!

By accident I now found Hazen's brigade—or what remained of it—which had made a half-mile march to add itself to the unrouted at the memorable Snodgrass Hill. Hazen's first remark to me was an inquiry about that artillery ammunition that he had sent me for.

It was needed badly enough, as were other kinds: for the last hour or two of that interminable day Granger's were the only men that had enough ammunition to make a five minutes' fight. Had the Confederates made one more general attack we should have had to meet them with the bayonet alone. I don't know why they did not; probably they were short of ammunition. I know, though, that while the sun was taking its own time to set we lived through the agony of at least one death each, waiting for them to come on.

At last it grew too dark to fight. Then away to our left and rear some of Bragg's people set up "the rebel yell." It was taken up successively and passed round to our front, along our right and in behind us again, until it seemed almost to have got to the point whence it started. It was the ugliest sound that any mortal ever heard—even a mortal exhausted and unnerved by two days of hard fighting, without sleep, without rest, without food and without hope. There was, however, a space somewhere at the back of us across which that horrible yell did not prolong itself; and through that we finally retired in profound silence and dejection, unmolested.

To those of us who have survived the attacks of both

Bragg and Time, and who keep in memory the dear dead comrades whom we left upon that fateful field, the place means much. May it mean something less to the younger men whose tents are now pitched where, with bended heads and clasped hands, God's great angels stood invisible among the heroes in blue and the heroes in gray, sleeping their last sleep in the woods of Chickamauga.

On Black Soldiering

First published in the San Francisco Examiner, June 5, 1898.

A skeptical correspondent asks me for an opinion of the fighting qualities of our colored regiments. Really I had thought the question settled long ago. The Negro will fight and fight well. From the time when we began to use him in civil war, through all his service against Indians on the frontier, to this day he has not failed to acquit himself acceptable to his White officers. I the more cheerfully testify to this because I was at one time a doubter. Under a general order from the headquarters of the Army, or possibly from the War Department, I once in a burst of ambition applied for rank as a field officer of colored troops, being then a line officer of white troops. Before my application was acted on I had repented and persuaded myself that the darkies would not fight; so when ordered to report to the proper board of officers, with a view to gratification of my wish, I "backed out" and secured "influence" which enabled me to remain in my humbler station. But at the battle of Nashville it was borne in upon me that I had made a fool of myself. During the two days of that memorable engagement the only reverse sustained by our arms was in an assault upon Overton Hill, a fortified salient of the Confederate line on the second day. The troops repulsed were a brigade of Beatty's division and a colored brigade of raw troops which had been brought up from a camp of instruction at Chattanooga. I was serving on

Gen. Beatty's staff, but was not doing duty that day, being disabled by a wound -- just sitting in the saddle and looking on. Seeing the darkies going in on our left I was naturally interested and observed them closely. Better fighting was never done. The front of the enemy's earthworks was protected by an intricate abatis of felled trees denuded of their foliage and twigs. Through this obstacle a cat would have made slow progress; its passage by troops under fire was hopeless from the first -- even the inexperienced black chaps must have known that. They did not hesitate a moment: their long lines swept into that fatal obstruction in perfect order and remained there as long as those of the white veterans on their right. And as many of them in proportion remained until borne away and buried after the action. It was as pretty an example of courage and discipline as one could wish to see. In order that my discomfiture and humiliation might lack nothing of completeness I was told afterward that one of their field officers succeeded in forcing his horse through a break in the abatis and was shot to rags on the slope on the parapet. But for my abjuration of faith in the Negroes' fighting qualities I might perhaps have been so fortunate as to be that man!

A Bivouac of the Dead

First published in 1903.

Away up in the heart of the Allegheny mountains, in Pocahontas county, West Virginia, is a beautiful little valley through which flows the east fork of the Greenbrier river. At a point where the valley road intersects the old Staunton and Parkersburg turnpike, a famous thoroughfare in its day, is a post office in a farm house. The name of the place is Travelers' Repose, for it was once a tavern. Crowning some low hills within a stone's throw of the house are long lines of old Confederate fortifications, skilfully designed and so well "preserved" that an hour's work by a brigade would put them into serviceable shape for the next civil war. This place had its battle—what was called a battle in the "green and salad days" of the great rebellion. A brigade of Federal troops, the writer's regiment among them, came over Cheat mountain, fifteen miles to the westward, and, stringing its lines across the little valley, felt the enemy all day; and the enemy did a little feeling, too. There was a great cannonading, which killed about a dozen on each side; then, finding the place too strong for assault, the Federals called the affair a reconnaissance in force, and burying their dead withdrew to the more comfortable place whence they had come. Those dead now lie in a beautiful national cemetery at Grafton, duly registered, so far as identified, and companioned by other Federal dead gathered from the several camps and battlefields of West

Virginia. The fallen soldier (the word "hero" appears to be a later invention) has such humble honors as it is possible to give.

His part in all the pomp that fills
The circuit of the Summer hills
Is that his grave is green

True, more than a half of the green graves in the Grafton cemetery are marked "Unknown," and sometimes it occurs that one thinks of the contradiction involved in "honoring the memory" of him of whom no memory remains to honor; but attempt seems to do no great harm to the living, even to the logical.

A few hundred yards to the rear of the old Confederate earthworks is a wooded hill. Years ago it was not wooded. Here, among the trees and in the undergrowth, are rows of shallow depressions, discoverable by removing the accumulated forest leaves. From some of them may be taken (and reverently replaced) small then slabs of the split stone of the country, with rude and reticent inscriptions by comrades. I found only one with a date, only one with full names of man and regiment. The entire number found was eight.

In these forgotten graves rest the Confederate dead—between eighty and one hundred, as nearly as can be made out. Some fell in the "battle;" the majority died of disease. Two, only two, have apparently been disinterred for reburial at their homes. So neglected and obscure in this campo santo that only he upon whose farm it is –the aged postmaster of Travelers' Repose—appears to know about it. Men living within a mile have never heard of it. Yet other men must be still living who assisted to lay these Southern soldiers where they are, and could identify some of the graves. Is there a man, North or South, who would begrudge the expense of giving to these fallen brothers the tribute of green graves? One would rather not think so. True, there are several hundreds of such places still discoverable in the track of the great war. All the stronger is the dumb-demand – the silent plea of these fallen brothers to what is "likest God within the soul."

They were honest and courageous foemen, having little in common with the political madmen who persuaded them to their doom and the literary bearers of false witness in the aftertime. They did not live through the period of honorable strife into the period of vilification—did not pass from the iron age to the brazen—from the era of the sword to that of the tongue and pen. Among them is no member of the Southern Historical Society. Their valor was not the fury of the non-combatant; they have no voice in the thunder of the civilians and the shouting. Not by them are impaired the dignity and infinite pathos of the Lost Cause. Give them, these blameless gentlemen, their rightful part in all the pomp that fills the circuit of the summer hills.

CPSIA information can be obtained
at www.ICGtesting.com
Printed in the USA
LVHW041240100520
655302LV00005B/1636